EXPOSED!

2011

ALISON JACKSON

EXPOSED!

The Pictures the Celebs Didn't Want You to See!

2011

CANONGATE

Edinburgh · London · New York · Melbourne

First published in Great Britain in 2011 by
Canongate Books Ltd, 14 High Street, Edinburgh EH1 1TE

1

www.canongate.tv

British Library Cataloguing-in-Publication Data
A catalogue record for this book is available on
request from the British Library

ISBN 978 0 85786 350 8

Design by Crown4to

Printed and bound in Italy by Graphicom

HELL'S STITCHING!

RAMSAY'S BOTOX BLUFF

IT BUST BE LOVE!

RANDY GRAY!

RANDY ANDY GETS THE SAC

THE REFUSE
COLLECTION

FULL BR

**OLD
LADY
GAGA**

SMELL-TON JOHN

NAPPY MAN

ZACH'S MY *BOY!*

MARRIED BRAND SWAPS SEX FOR GARDENING

HUT STUFF!

TOOL SHED!

GADDAFI: NO SURRENDER, WE'RE NOT WOMEN

FEELING THE HEAT

LOOKS TO DI FOR

FIT FOR A
QUEEN

BROOD
PITT

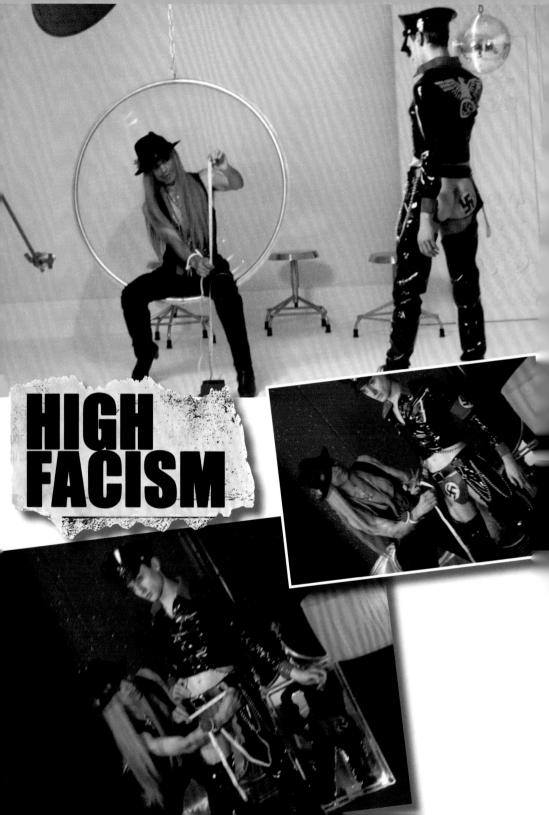

HIGH
FACISM

MARCHING ORDERS
LEFT, REICH, LEFT, REICH, LEFT, REICH

KATE: I'M NO BRIDEOREXIC

MINE'S A CHICKEN ROYALE!

SEX MA-SHEEN

CHARLIE AND HIS ANGELS

HARRY PLANS
'QUIET' STAG DO FOR WILLS

TROLLEYED!

KATE
COPS
AN
EYEFUL

ONE L
OF A
NIGHT

CLEGG – I'M RIGHT BEHIND YOU

SLEAZY TIGER

IT'S GRRRRREAT!

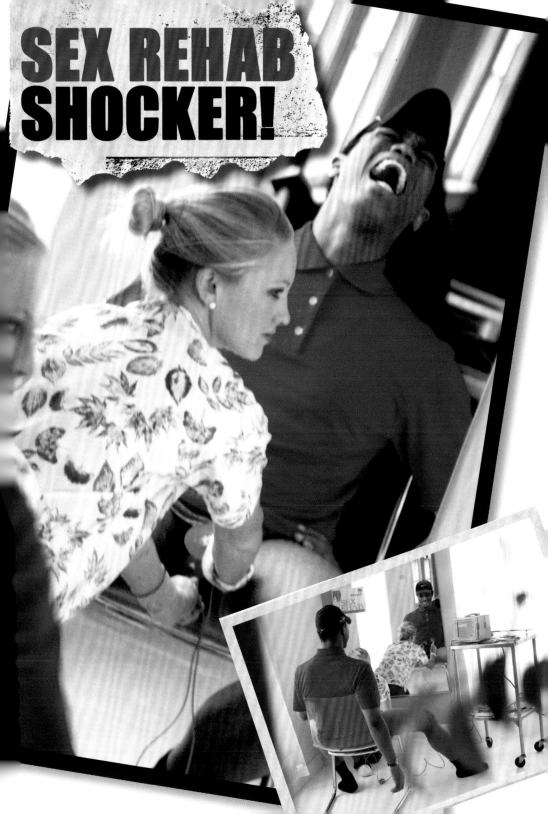

SEX REHAB SHOCKER!

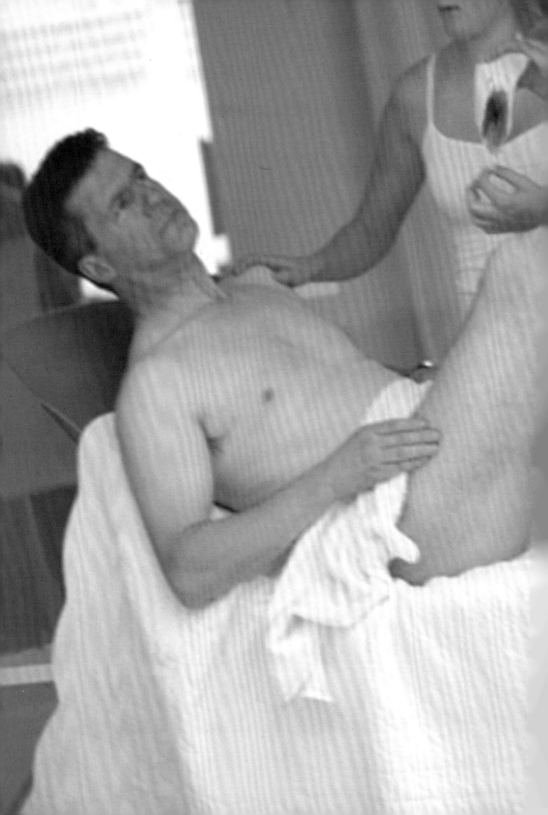

WAX FACTOR

SIMON C-OWWWWWELL!

HOMO

GADDAFI
PREPARES TO FIGHT TO DEATH

SEXTRA TIME FOR GIGGSY

CENTREF-OLD TRAFFORD

A BIT OF ALL WHITE!

PRINCELY PREPARATIONS

BECK 'EM DEAD!

KATE'S CAKE DATE

FLIRTY HARRY

IN LINE TO THE THRONE

LET'S
DANCE

BUCKS
FIZZ

HEIR TODAY, GONE TOMORROW

CROWNING
GLORY

The Royal
BEDDING ...

MORNING AFTER
THE WEDDING BEFORE

MILITARY
MANOEUVRES

ARE HARRY AND PIPPA NEXT?

PIPPA'S WEAPON OF

MASS DISTRACTION

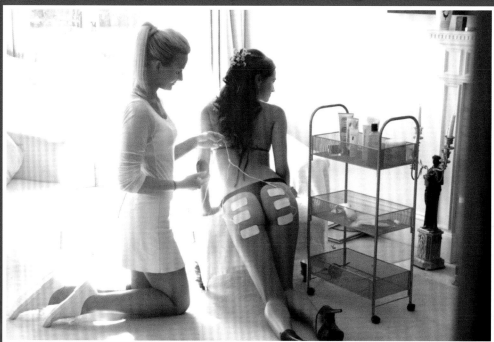

NEVER GUNNER FIND ME!

OSAMA BIN
HARD-ON

DYEING
FOR
HIS
CAUSE

**WHEN
OBAMA
GOT
OSAMA**

KISSA
MIDDLETON

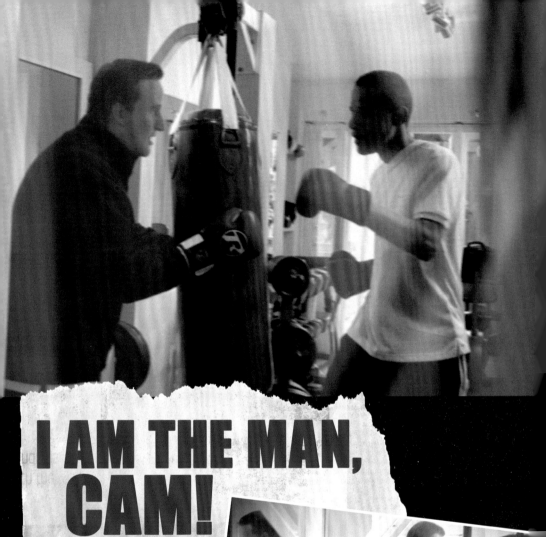

I AM THE MAN, CAM!

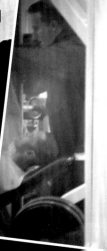

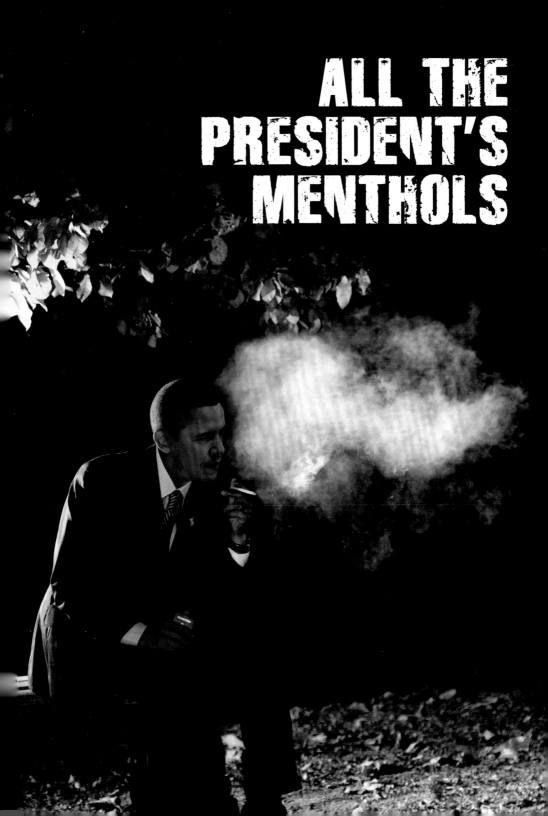

ALL THE PRESIDENT'S MENTHOLS

PORKER FACE

SIMON'S HIT LIST

CHEZZA SCISSOR SHOCKER!

YOU PLONKER!

NO GO
FOR MILIBAND
BROMANCE

ED
LOCK!

BRUSH
OFF!

SIMON
SAYS ...

Sorry

PAIN ROONEY

THATCH OF THE DAY

PLANNING
A-HEAD

POOL
IS FORGIVEN

LAST CHANCE *for ASH*

ROUND OF MEETINGS

DEPU-TIE PRIME MINISTER

READY
TO POP

Beck to the Drawing Board

'Can't we just call her Jane?'

KATE: MINE'S A LARGE ONE

WEE BIT DRUNK?

KATE'S BIG FAT TIPSY WEDDING

PORTALOO

WIMBLE-DONE!

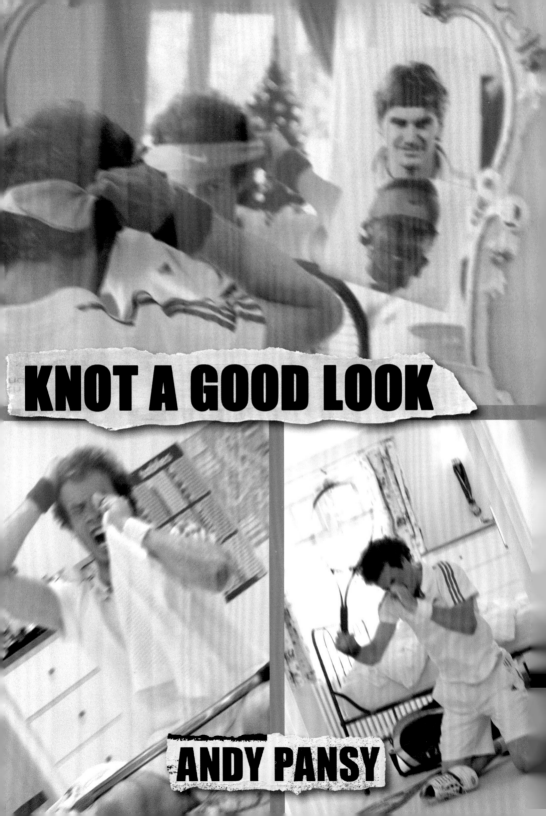

KNOT A GOOD LOOK

ANDY PANSY

MURRAY
MADNESS

STAR'S SECRET BATTLE
WITH BOOZE

ORDER
OF THE
PEE-NIX

HARRY POTTER AND THE PHILOSOPHER'S CONE

CROUCHING WENDI

WEN WIVES
ATTACK!

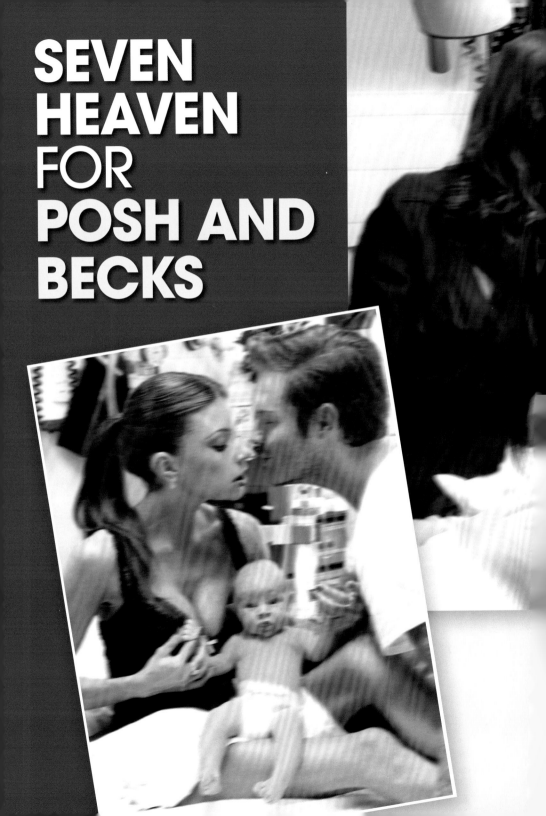

SEVEN HEAVEN FOR POSH AND BECKS

POSH'S
Little Princess

How We Named
OUR LITTLE GIRL

FLUSH OF
INSPIRATION

BECKS FEEDING

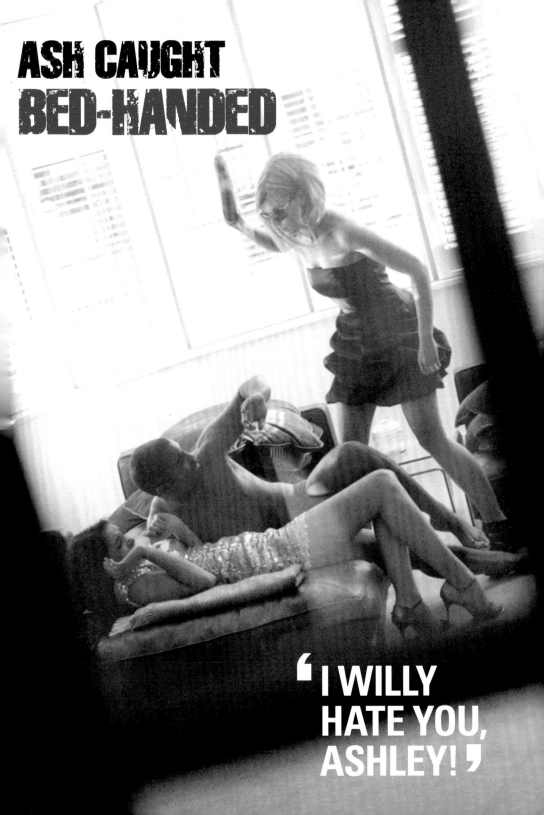

ASH CAUGHT BED-HANDED

' I WILLY HATE YOU, ASHLEY! '

LIBYA 1 – 1 LONDON

KEEP CAM AND CARRY ON

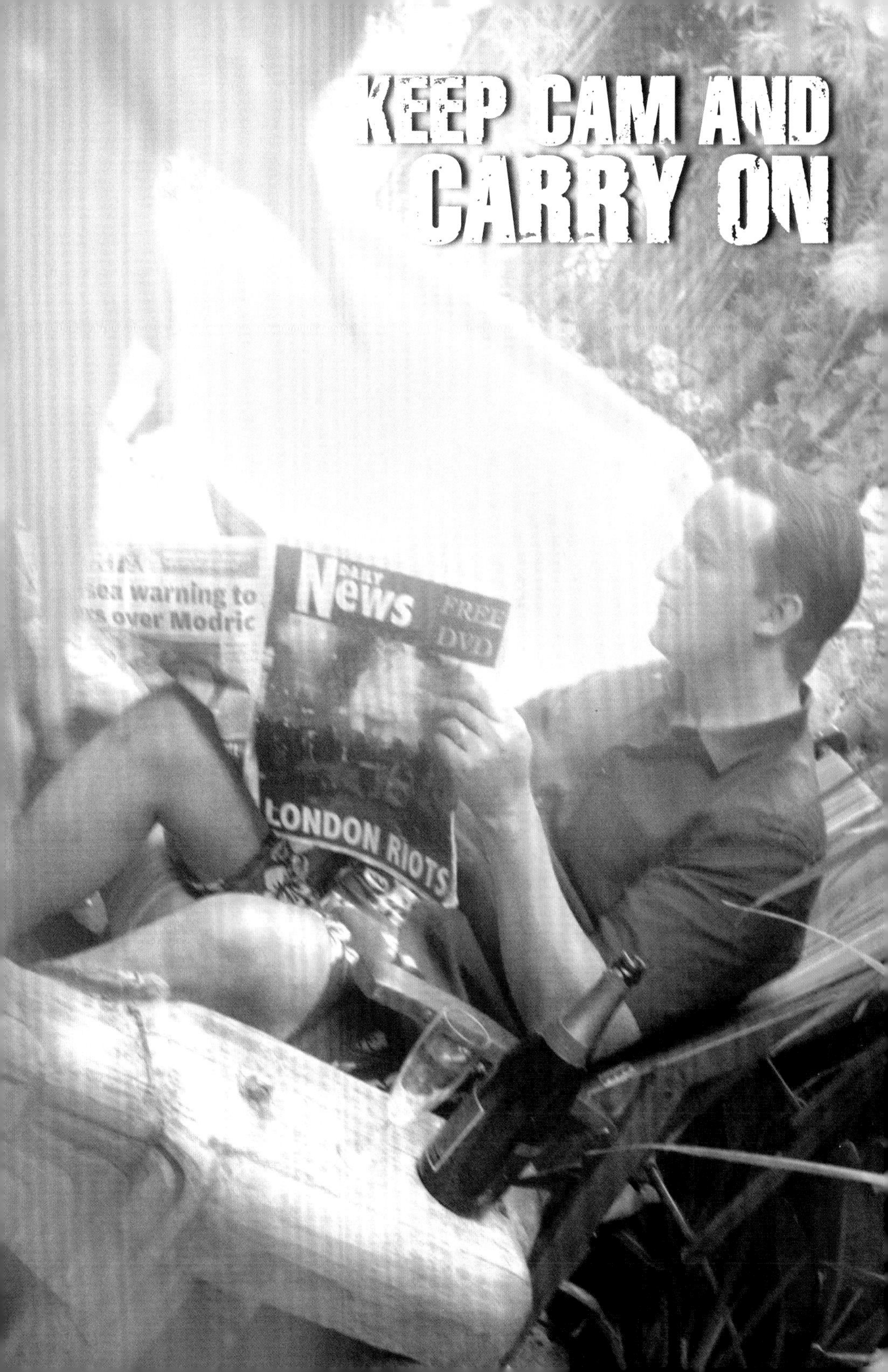

GADDAFLEE

A CUPPA MORE YEARS YET . . .

HARRY BIRTHDAY TO YOU ...

TRASHLEY

WORMS HIS WAY BACK IN AGAIN

HEIR'S HOW
ONE DOES IT

KATE'S LATE!

KING SIZE?

Stocking FRILLERS

NAPPY CHRISTMAS

BARKINGHAM PALACE!

GOLDEN POOLS!

YOU
MUST BE
CHOKING!

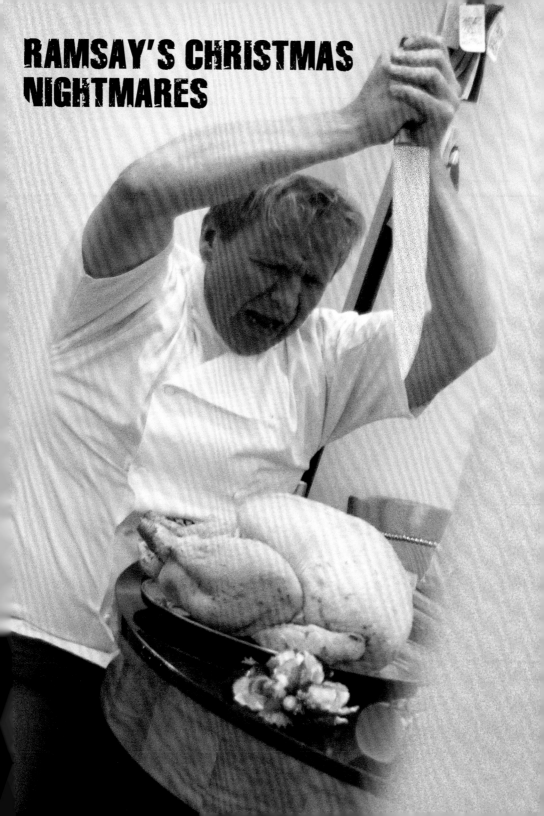

RAMSAY'S CHRISTMAS NIGHTMARES

RYAN'S
LITTLE
HELPERS

. . . AND A
HARRY NEW YEAR

Acknowledgements

A review of topical events is something I have wanted to do for many years, and I would like to thank everyone who has worked so hard and fast, and with incredible attention to detail, to help put this book together.

A big thank you to my publisher, Canongate, to my editor, Jenny Lord, and to Nick Davies for their help in turning the idea of an annual-in-pictures into a reality. A very special thank you must also go to my agent, Robert Kirby at United Agents.

I am indebted to Tom Rawstorne for his essential and continued creative input and editorial support. Without him and his ideas for the photographs this book would not have been completed. I also would like to thank Dave Masters and Luke Blackall.

A very big thank you to my highly creative production and post-production teams, who have worked fantastically hard to create the best images.

For production, thank you to Jennifer Davis and Harriet Collings, and to my researcher/AP, Hannah Lane. Also a big thank you to Charles Bennett and Kwesi McLoud.

For design and art direction, thank you to Charlotte Copeland, Melissa Aldrete lazo de la Vega, Jonathan Houghton Van Beek and their art department, Emily Todd and Louise Todd.

Thanks to my head of post-production and manager, Karin Gunnarsson; to my head of photography, Andrew Farrar; and to Daniel Swan and Andrew Tapper for retouching.

Thanks to my wonderfully skilled hair-and-make-up team: Terri Pace, Juliet Argent, Kelly Harrington, Mo Nabbach at M and M Hair Academy and Sunita Thompson; and to my costume team: Lenka Padysakova, Sarah Masters, Cat Yap and Maya Gigliola.

For cinematography and editing, thanks to Caroline Bridges, Rachael James and Giles Andrews. Thanks to Patrick Maxwell for editing the moving-picture version.

For camera assisting and lighting, thank you to Robert Radmall, Marie Ansolom and Gray Hutton. They kept me on track photographically and technically and ordered my thousands of shots – I shot over 200,000 images for this work, so no small task. And to Sascha Ramin for keeping it all arranged and stored.

I am indebted to The Susan Scott Agency and Nicci Topping Casting for all their casting help, and to Ana Vav at Limelight People and Venette Shantelle at Edge Models for supplying excellent actors and extras. Thanks to Michele at Fresh Locations and Lavish Locations.

And, of course, a big thank you to the stars of my photographs – the lookalikes.

Finally, thank you to Hamiltons Gallery, London, and M&B Gallery, Los Angeles.

Special thanks to:
www.thesundaytimes.co.uk for their ongoing support and for allowing the use of photographs originally commissioned by them.

Alison Jackson is an artist who explores the cult of celebrity. Using lookalikes, she makes realistic work about celebrities doing things in private; creating scenarios we have all imagined but never seen – the hot images the media can't get. Her work has been exhibited in galleries and museums across Europe and North America. She has made a number of shows for television, including the BAFTA Award-winning BBC series *Double Take*, and is the author of three previous books, *Confidential*, *Private* and *Up the Aisle*.
www.alisonjackson.com.